know
the
game

Basketball

Produced in collaboration with the
English Basket Ball Association

Published by A & C Black (Publishers) Ltd
35 Bedford Row, London WC1R 4JH

Contents

Foreword

Basketball, which is now the most widely played sport in the world, started in a humble way. In 1891 Dr James Naismith conceived the idea of a game when he was a student at the YMCA Training College at Springfield, Mass., USA. A peach-basket was erected at each end of the gymnasium and two teams were selected. The object was to get the football that was used into the opponents' basket, using only the hands.

The possibilities of the game soon became apparent and experience led to certain rules being drawn up for the good conduct of the game. It was not intended to permit tackling like rugby and consequently was made a no-contact sport. Moreover, the players were not allowed to take more than one pace while holding the ball. The chief feature of the game is that skilful play is more important than physical strength.

So extensive was the advance of Basketball that it was included in the 1936 Olympiad and is now an Olympic Sport for men and women. It is also one of the most popular spectator sports in the world.

Basketball is one of the most exhilarating of all games. It requires fitness, skill, dexterity, co-ordination, agility, alertness and the ability to co-operate with the other members of the team.

This book sets out in a simple form the rules of the game, the techniques of officiating and the basic playing skills, so that more people can enjoy the game of Basketball.

President
English Basket Ball Association

Equipment

The playing court

Basketball is played on a court marked out on a flat surface; grass courts are not allowed.

The standard dimensions of the court are 28 m (91 ft 6 ins) long and 15 m (49 ft 3 ins) wide. Variations of minus 4.00 m (13 ft) on length and 2.00 m (6 ft 6 ins) on width are permitted.

The playing court is marked by lines, which are clearly visible and 5 cm (2 in) in width.

The baskets

The baskets consist of rings and nets, one at each end of the playing court.

The ring is constructed from solid iron, 45 cm (18 in) in diameter and painted orange.

Nets are best made of white cord suspended from the rings and constructed so that they check the ball momentarily as it passes through the basket.

The ring is attached to the backboards in a horizontal plane and fixed 3.05 (10 ft) above the floor.

The backboards

The backboards originally installed were to prevent the ball going out of play and spectators interfering with play on a shot; they are now standard equipment required by the rules.

A backboard measures 1.8 m (6 ft) × 1.2 m (4 ft), and is usually made of smooth hard wood 3 cm (1 $\frac{3}{16}$ in) thick, but can be of a suitable transparent material.

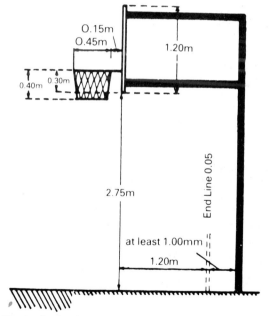

Fig. 1   Basket, backboard and support

3

The ball

The ball is spherical, made of a rubber bladder covered with a case of leather, rubber or synthetic material. It must be between 78 cm (30½ in) and 75 cm (29½ in) in circumference, with a weight of at least 600 g and not more than 650 g.

When inflated and dropped onto a solid wooden floor from a height of about 1.8 m (6 ft) it should rebound to a height of at least 1.2 m (4 ft) and not more than 1.4 m (4 ft 8 in) measured to the top of the ball. For a match the home team should provide at least one good used ball. Neither team may use the match ball for practice.

Clothing

The individual player's equipment is comparatively simple, the basic playing equipment being shorts and vests. The player will usually be provided with his vests and shorts by his club, so that members of the team wear identical kit. Each player must wear numbers on his vest, the one on the front 10 cm (4 in) high and the one on the back 20 cm (8 in) high. Numbers for International play range from 4 to 15, and, in addition, in England numbers 20–25, 30–35, 40–45 and 50–55 may be used.

Footwear is a very important part of the player's equipment. Basketball shoes are either low cut or high

Fig. 2   Playing Kit

cut depending upon the personal preference of the player. They should fit well and have a sole thick enough to cushion the jumping and landing that will occur in the game.

The game

The aim of each team is to throw the ball into its opponents' basket and to prevent the other team from securing the ball or scoring.

The game is started by a 'jump ball' at the centre when the referee throws the ball up.

When the ball is in play it may be passed, thrown, rolled, batted or dribbled in any direction. Both quick passing and/or dribbling are used to move the ball into a scoring position.

The game is stopped when certain rules are infringed. There are four important aspects of play controlled by the rules; these concern contact, progressing with the ball, dribbling, and certain time rules. Basketball, like other games, has rules concerning the method of starting play, restarting after a score and after a violation of the rules.

The court is divided by a half-way line, and that half of the court which contains the opponents' basket is referred to as a team's *front court*. The other half at the team's defensive end is their *back court*.

The game is divided into two halves of twenty minutes each, with a half-time interval of ten minutes. The game watch is stopped when the whistle is blown, so no playing time is lost during stoppages.

A game cannot end in a draw. An extra period of five minutes is played, plus as many extra periods as are necessary to break the tie.

The teams

The game is played by two teams. Each team can consist of up to ten players, five players from each team being on court during the match. The others are substitutes and can be substituted at certain times in the game (see p. 18).

Each team has a coach who is responsible for his team's tactical play, supplying the names and numbers of his players to the scorer before the match and, when he decides to request a substitution, instructing the substitute to report to the scorer.

Starting play

Play is started by a jump ball at the centre circle.

Jump ball

One member of each team stands in the circle, on either side of the line marked across the circle.

All other players must remain outside the restraining circle until the ball has been touched by one of the jumpers.

The referee tosses the ball up between the two players to a height greater than the players can reach by jumping. After the ball has reached its highest point the jumpers may tap it in any direction, while it is on its downward flight.

The jumpers may not leave their position until one of

them has touched the ball. Neither of them may tap the ball more than twice; and the player who has touched it twice may not do so again until it has touched one of the other players, the basket or the backboard, or the floor.

Fig. 3   Jump ball at the start of play

In play

A player may:

- catch, control, pass or shoot the ball with either or both hands. He must not hit the ball with clenched fist or deliberately play the ball with his foot, although accidentally striking the ball with the foot or leg is not a violation

- dribble the ball by throwing, batting, bouncing or rolling it. The ball must always touch the floor before he touches it again. A player is entitled to a dribble each time he gains control of the ball. The dribble ends when he touches the ball with both hands at once or allows it to rest in either or both hands. Having ended his dribble, he may not begin another dribble until he has taken a shot, or the ball has been played by another player

Fig. 4   Dribbling past a defender

- if the ball was received while standing still, carry it for one complete pace, but not for two or more paces. If the ball was received on the run, he may carry it for one pace, i.e. a step with one foot and then a step with the other foot before passing or shooting

- shoot and score from any point in the court
- pivot with the ball in his hands. That is, he can step once or more in any direction with one foot while turning on the other, which must stay on the floor at its point of contact.

Fig. 4b

Progression with the ball

When a player wants to advance with the ball he may dribble, i.e. bounce the ball to the ground with one hand.

To stop legally a player must execute the stop within the limits of two steps, one with each foot. The rules specify clearly the limits within which a player may stop, and then pivot when carrying the ball. These limits are defined by a two count rhythm, i.e. the step with one foot and then the other. The limits are:

● A player who receives the ball while standing still may pivot using either foot as the pivot foot.

● A player who receives the ball while he is progressing or upon completion of a dribble may use a two count rhythm in coming to a stop or getting rid of the ball.

The **first count** occurs:

(a) as he receives the ball if either foot is touching the floor at the time he receives it, or

(b) as either foot touches the floor or as both feet touch the floor simultaneously after he receives the ball, if both feet are off the floor when he receives it.

The **second count** occurs when, after the count of one, either foot touches the floor or both feet touch the floor simultaneously.

Fig. 5 Stride stop

When a player comes to a legal stop, if one foot is in advance of the other, he may pivot, but only on the one count foot (usually the rear).

- A player who receives the ball while standing still, or who comes to a legal stop while holding the ball:

(a) may lift the pivot foot or jump when he throws for goal or passes, but the ball must leave his hands before one or both feet again touch the floor;

(b) may not lift the pivot foot, in starting a dribble before the ball leaves his hands.

To progress with the ball in excess of the limits is a violation of the rules.

To play within these rules there are two methods used by players to stop when receiving a pass whilst moving or when finishing a dribble; these are a jump stop and a stride stop. In a jump stop the player takes the ball in the air and stops, landing on both feet simultaneously. With the stride stop the player uses a full place to stop. Having caught the ball when both feet are off the ground the player lands on one foot and then steps forward on the other.

Fig. 6 Jump stop

Time rules

30 seconds A team in control of the ball must make a try for basket within 30 seconds of having gained control.

10 seconds When a team gains control of the ball in its back court it must cause the ball to go into the front court within 10 seconds.

A player must not cause the ball to go into his team's back court when he is in the front court. This restriction applies to all situations including throw-in from out-of-bounds, rebounds, and interceptions. It does not apply, however, to the situation when a team has a throw-in from out-of-bounds from the mid-point on the side line when the captain uses his option of taking possession instead of free throws, or following a coach technical foul (p. 16) or intentional foul (p. 15).

5 seconds On a throw-in from out-of-bounds a player must within 5 seconds throw, bounce or roll the ball to another player within the court. When the ball has been placed at the disposal of a player to attempt a free throw he must throw the ball within 5 seconds. The 5 seconds count is started when the ball is at the disposal of the player and finishes when he releases the ball or the whistle is blown because he has exceeded the 5 seconds.

When any single player who is closely guarded is holding the ball and does not pass, shoot, bat, roll or dribble the ball within 5 seconds, this is a violation and the ball is awarded to the opposing team.

3 seconds A player shall not remain in his opponents' restricted area for more than 3 seconds when he or his team has control of the ball. This restriction is in force for all out-of-bounds situations, but does not apply while the ball is in the air on a try for goal or during a rebound from the backboard. Allowance may be made for a player who has been in the restricted area for less than 3 seconds and dribbles in to shoot for goal.

Fouls

A personal foul is a player foul which involves contact with an opponent. A technical foul is an infringement against the spirit of the rules or the use of unsportsman-like tactics.

Personal fouls

It is the duty of every player on court to avoid contact. If contact occurs a personal foul is awarded against the player whom the official considers to be primarily responsible.

Every player on court is entitled to occupy any part of the court not occupied by an opponent, provided that he does not cause any personal contact in obtaining that position. A player is considered to occupy not only the part of the floor covered by his feet, but, in addition, a 'cylinder' between the floor and the roof with a base

Fig. 7   Illegal contact by player No. 6

roughly equivalent to the player's body dimensions. Should an opponent run or reach into this cylinder and cause contact, then he is responsible for that contact. If the player in extending his arm or leg outside his cylinder causes contact, then he is responsible for that contact. It is legal for a player to extend his arm or leg, but should an opponent wish to move by, then the extended limb must be withdrawn.

The mere fact that the defensive player is attempting to play the ball does not justify him in making contact with the player in possession of the ball. If the defensive player causes personal contact in an attempt to get at the ball from an unfavourable position, he should be penalised.

When players are stationary it is relatively easy for a referee to make a correct judgement as to which player is responsible for any contact that may occur, but it is more difficult when the players are moving. The rules of the game differentiate between a dribbler and a player who does not have the ball. A dribbler is expected to be in full control and be able to stop, change direction, pass or shoot in a split second. A dribbler should expect that defenders will move into his path at any time and should be prepared to take any action necessary to avoid contact. Until the dribbler gets his head and shoulders past the opponent the greater responsibility for contact remains with the dribbler. Contact by a dribbler on the front of the defensive player will usually result in the foul being called on the dribbler. Should the contact be by the defender on the side of the dribbler, then the foul should be called on the defensive player. Providing the defender can establish a legal defensive position (i.e. with both feet on the floor and facing the dribbler, in the path of the movement of the dribbler), then should contact occur the dribbler is responsible for this contact. Once the defensive position is established the dribbler must be prepared to avoid contact. A defender, providing he has gained his position first, does not have to give the dribbler time and distance in which to stop.

When defending against a player who does not have the ball, the defender must give a moving opponent time and distance in which to stop or change direction. A player must not move into the path of an opponent without the ball so quickly that he cannot stop or change direction.

A player may not contact an opponent with his hand, unless such contact is only with the opponent's hand while it is on the ball and is incidental to an attempt to play the ball. The rules give special protection to a player taking a shot and even contact with the hand of the shooter is penalised with a foul.

Judgement of personal fouls

The referee, having judged that contact has occurred and blown the whistle, then has to make a judgement as to the severity of the foul. These cover a *normal personal foul*, an *intentional foul* and a *disqualifying foul*. The normal personal foul can be looked upon as a mistake by the player, an error in skill that caused the contact. An intentional foul is contact that results when a player makes no effort to avoid contact, when he intentionally disregards the ball and causes personal contact. A disqualifying foul is a flagrant unsportsmanlike foul, e.g. a punch.

Due to the different penalties involved, the official has to decide if the foul was committed on a player in the *act of shooting* or not.

A *double foul* is a situation where two opponents commit personal fouls against each other at approximately the same time.

Fig. 8a   Normal personal foul

Fig. 8b   Intentional foul

13

A *multiple foul* is when a player is fouled by two or more opponents at approximately the same time.

Fig. 8e   Foul on a player in the act of shooting

Fig. 8c   Disqualifying foul

Fig. 8f   Multiple foul

Fig. 8d   Double foul

Penalty for personal foul

When an official blows his whistle for a personal foul, he indicates the player who has committed the foul. This player has the foul charged against him, i.e. recorded on the scoresheet. The offender must raise his arm and turn to face the scorer's table, so that the scorer may record the foul correctly. For failing to do this, the offending player, after being warned once by an official, may have a technical foul charged against him. A player who has committed five fouls, personal or technical, must leave the court.

Penalties—Foul charged against each offender plus the following additional penalty for:

Normal personal foul

The non-offending team is given the ball for a throw-in from out-of-bounds at the side line nearest the place of the foul. However, when a team has committed seven player fouls, personal or technical, in a half, all other fouls committed are penalised by one plus one free throws (unless the team committing the foul is in control of the ball in which case the penalty is the same as before the seven fouls had been committed).

Foul on a player in the act of shooting

1. If the goal is made, it shall count (2 or 3 points) and, in addition, one free throw shall be awarded.
2. If the goal is missed, two or three free throws will be awarded.

Intentional and disqualifying fouls

Two free throws are awarded to the non-offending team except when a goal is scored by the offended player (see above). After the free throws, whether successful or not, the ball is put into play at mid-court side line by a member of the free thrower's team. For a disqualifying foul the player must leave the game immediately.

Double foul

No free throws are awarded, and the ball is brought into play at the nearest circle by a jump ball between the two players involved.

Multiple foul

The offended player is awarded two free throws except if he was in the act of shooting (see above).

Right of option

A team that has been awarded two or three, or one plus one, free throws shall have the option either of attempting the throws or of putting the ball in play from out-of-bounds at the mid-point of a side line. The decision shall rest with the captain of the team.

Technical fouls

Technical fouls are offences against the spirit of the game, but some, which are obviously unintentional and have no effect on the play, or are of an administrative nature, are not considered technical fouls unless there is repetition after a warning by an official. Technical infractions which are deliberate, or unsportsmanlike, or which give the offender an unfair advantage, are penalised immediately with a technical foul.

A player shall not disregard warnings by an official or use unsportsmanlike actions such as:

● delaying the game by preventing the ball from being put promptly into play

- baiting an opponent or obstructing his opponent's vision by waving his hands close to his opponent's eyes
- using profanity or disrespectfully addressing an official
- not raising his arm properly when charged with a foul
- changing his number without telling the scorer and the referee
- entering the court as a substitute without reporting first to the scorer and then to an official
- grasping the ring.

Fig. 9   Technical foul

Penalty for a player technical foul

Each offence will be charged as a foul against the offender and two free throws awarded to the opponents or the option of a throw-in from the mid-point side line.

The captain shall designate the thrower. For infractions which are persistent or flagrant a player shall be disqualified.

Technical foul by coach or substitute

The coach, assistant coach or substitute player may not enter the court without permission. Neither may they leave their places to follow the action on the court nor disrespectfully address officials (including Table officials) or opponents.

Here again a distinction is made between unintentional and deliberate infractions by coaches or substitutes.

During a charged time-out a coach may address his players, including substitutes. The coach may also direct and encourage his team during the game from the bench.

Penalty

Each offence by the coach shall be recorded and two free throws awarded to the opponents. After the free throws, whether successful or not, the ball is put into play, at mid-court side line, by a member of the free thrower's team. Persistent or flagrant infractions may cause the coach to be banished from the vicinity of the court. The assistant coach or, if none, the captain, would then replace him.

Free throws

A free throw for a personal foul is awarded to the player who was fouled, unless he is disqualified for any reason, or injured. To take the free throw the thrower stands immediately behind (not on) the free throw line.

Fig. 10   Free throw

Nobody—not even an official—may stand inside the free throw lane when a player is taking a free throw. The other players may line up along the sides of the lane, in the spaces marked, during a free throw (except following a coach technical foul or intentional or disqualifying foul). The spaces nearest the basket are for two players of the defending team, with the other players taking alternate positions.

The free thrower is allowed a maximum of 5 seconds

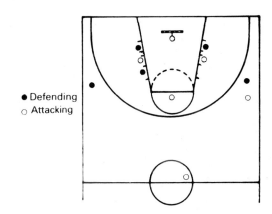

● Defending
○ Attacking

Fig. 11   During a free throw each player positions himself according to the tactics adopted by his team

to take his shot. Neither the thrower nor any other player may touch the line or the floor in the free throw lane until the ball touches the ring or until it is apparent that it will not touch it. These are violations.

The one and one rule is a special situation and is applied when a player of the team not in control of the ball commits a subsequent personal foul after his team has committed seven player fouls in a half. The player against whom the foul has been committed is given one free throw; if it is successful the player takes a second free throw. If the first throw is unsuccessful play continues.

17

Substitutions

Any or all of the five players in action may be replaced by substitutes during the game. This is done on instructions by the team's coach. The coach should send the substitute—who must be ready to play—to the scorer. After reporting to the scorer, the substitute must sit on the seat provided until the scorer sounds his signal. He should then stand up and indicate to the nearest floor official that he wishes to enter the court. He should not enter the court until beckoned to do so by an official, whereupon he should enter the court without delay.

Substitutions can only be made when the ball is 'dead' and the game clock stopped.

Following a violation, only the team which has possession of the ball for the throw-in from out-of-bounds may effect a substitution. If this occurs the opponents also may effect a substitution.

Both teams may substitute when a foul or a jump ball is called, but, should the team wish to substitute when free throws have been awarded, this must take place before the first throw is taken. The player taking the free throw may be substituted provided the request was made before the first throw and that his last throw was successful; in this case the opponents may be granted one substituton.

If a player is injured and in danger the officials can stop the game immediately. Otherwise the officials wait until the play has been completed, i.e. the team in possession of the ball has thrown for goal, has lost possession of the ball, has withheld the ball from play, or the ball has become a dead ball, before the game is stopped. If the injured player cannot continue to play he shall be substituted within one minute, and the substitute takes any free throws or his place at the jump ball.

Charged time-out

Two charged time-outs may be granted to each team during each half of playing time, and one charged time-out for each extra period. A time-out is of one minute's duration and gives an opportunity for the coach to change tactics and give instructions to his players. A request for a charged time-out can be granted when the ball is dead and the game clock is stopped, or following a field goal scored by the opponents of the team who has made the request.

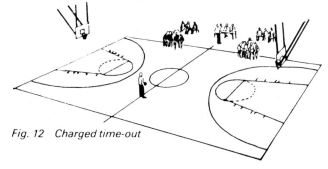

Fig. 12   Charged time-out

Out-of-bounds

The ball is out-of-bounds:

(a) when it touches a player who is out-of-bounds, i.e. a player touching the floor on or outside the boundary line, and that player is held responsible;

(b) when it touches any other person, the floor or any object on or outside the boundary, or the supports or back of the backboard. It is considered to have been put out-of-bounds by the player who last touched it;

(c) if a player deliberately throws or taps the ball onto an opponent thus causing it to go out-of-bounds, the ball shall be awarded to the opponents even though it was last touched by that team.

An official then indicates the team which is to put the ball into play. A player from this team standing out-of-bounds, on or behind the boundary line near where the ball left the court, must, within five seconds from the time the ball is at his disposal, throw, bounce or roll it to another player within the court, from out-of-bounds at the side near where the ball left the court.

When the ball is awarded to a team out-of-bounds at the side line in its front court, an official must hand the ball to the player who is to put it in play. This is to clarify the decision and not delay the game.

While the ball is being passed into the court, every other player must be completely inside the court.

Note—if the ball goes out-of-bounds
(a) after being touched simultaneously by two opponents
(b) and the official is in doubt as to who last touched it
(c) and the officials disagree
play is restarted by a jump ball between the two players concerned for (a), and for any two opponents for (b) and (c) at the nearest restraining circle.

Held ball

This may be declared:

● when two or more rival players of opposing teams have one or both hands firmly on the ball, so that neither of them can get it away without using 'undue roughness';

● when the ball lodges in the basket supports.

Fig. 13   Held ball

After calling a held ball, the referee then orders a jump ball. This takes place at the centre of the nearest restraining circle.

Restarting play

The method of starting play after fouls and held balls has been described. For other violations of the rules the ball is awarded to the non-offending team for a throw-in from the nearest point at the side line out-of-bounds.

After a field goal (see below), play is restarted by an opponent of the scoring team by throwing the ball into court from behind the end line where the goal was scored.

Scoring

Scoring is by a system of points.

Two or three points are awarded for a 'goal from the field', i.e. when the ball enters the basket from above as a result of ordinary play. Two points will normally be awarded for a field goal, unless the shot is taken from outside the marked semi-circle (6.25 metres from the basket) when 3 points are awarded.

One point is awarded for a goal by a free throw.

If a team refuses to continue to play after being so ordered by the referee it forfeits the game. The opponents are credited with a 2–0 win unless they were leading at the time of forfeit, when the score stands.

If a defensive player touches the ball when it is on its downward flight during a shot for basket, or touches the ring of backboard while the ball is on the ring during a try for goal, or the basket when the ball is in the basket, this is interference and the shooter will be awarded a goal for his shot.

Control of the game

Officials

The officials are a referee and an umpire who are assisted by a scorer and a timekeeper and, in top-class games, a 30-second operator.

The referee and umpire are required to wear a uniform consisting of long grey trousers, a grey shirt and basket-ball shoes.

The referee and umpire jointly conduct the game according to the rules.
Their duties include:

● putting the ball into play
● stopping play when the ball is dead
● ordering time-out
● beckoning substitutes on to the court
● passing the ball to a player for a specified throw from a prescribed position
● silently counting seconds to administer certain time rules (see p.11)

The officials are responsible for imposing penalties for breaches of the rules and for unsportsmanlike conduct.

Play is stopped by one of the officials blowing a whistle when a decision has to be made known, usually through the use of an official signal.

The referee is the senior official and is responsible for:

- inspection and approval of all equipment
- tossing the ball at the centre to start play
- deciding whether a goal shall count if the officials disagree
- a team's forfeiture of a game when conditions warrant it
- deciding questions on which the timekeeper and scorer disagree
- examining the score sheet and approving the score at the end of each half
- making decisions on any points not covered by the rules.

The 30-second operator is required to operate the device for timing 30 seconds. However, when there is no such device this duty is undertaken by the trailing official (see p. 23).

Refereeing technique

The basic responsibility of the basketball officials is to have the game played with as little interference as possible on their part. It is the purpose of the rules to penalise a player who by reason of an illegal act has placed his opponents at a disadvantage. To be able to undertake his responsibility a good official (referee or umpire) must:

- know the rules of the game
- be in the right place
- be looking at the right part of the court

The referee and umpire control the game by a division of duties and by co-operating so that they watch all of the play and all of the players. To do this they use a system of double officiating. The officials work on

Fig. 14   Referee in action

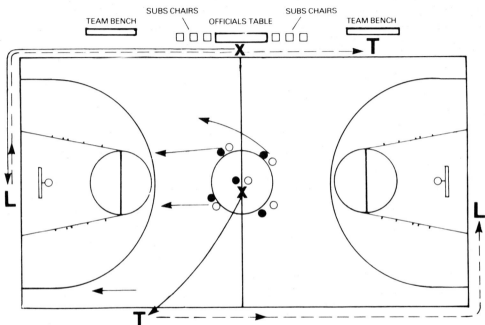

TEAM BENCH · SUBS CHAIRS · OFFICIALS TABLE · SUBS CHAIRS · TEAM BENCH

FIG.15

After the jump ball with play going to the left, the direction of the movement of officials to take up 'Leading' (L) and 'Trailing' (T) positions is indicated. When play moves to the opposite end of court their movement is indicated by the broken lines

opposite sides of the court, each official being responsible for the side line nearest to him, and the end line and the free throw lane to his right. Before each jump ball and after each foul the officials change sides of the court. During normal floor play the officials do not try to keep level with ball as any quick movement of the ball would leave them both behind play and in a bad position to see what is happening on court.

The officials endeavour to 'sandwich' the ball between them with one of them always ahead of the play (the leading official) and the other behind the play (the trailing official). During the game each official moves to his right ahead of play (leading) and to his left behind the play (trailing). While play is developing, the leading official will find he is primarily responsible for play away from the ball, e.g. he looks for contact as players manoeuvre for position, and 3 seconds violation, whilst the trailing official will find he is primarily concerned with the ball and players around it. Each official will blow for and penalise any infringements he sees anywhere on court.

As far as possible the officials should keep off the court and their normal lines of movement to their observation areas should be outside the side and end lines. They may 'cut the corners' as either leading or trailing official if they need to do so, provided they *in no way* interfere with the movement of the ball or the players on the court. It is normally only for 'fast breaks' that the officials need to cut the corners in order to keep up with the play. In such cases it is unlikely that there will be anyone in the corners of the court with whom they might interfere. It is permissible for the official to station himself on court if by so doing he can better observe the play and the players. He should do so only while bearing in mind that he must in no way impede the play, and that his normal position is outside the court.

Officials' signals

The officials use a number of hand signals to indicate their decisions to players, the table officials and spectators.

Fig. 16 Signals

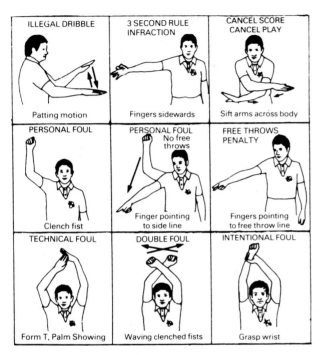

ILLEGAL DRIBBLE	**3 SECOND RULE INFRACTION**	**CANCEL SCORE CANCEL PLAY**
Patting motion	Fingers sidewards	Sift arms across body
PERSONAL FOUL	**PERSONAL FOUL** No free throws	**FREE THROWS PENALTY**
Clench fist	Finger pointing to side line	Fingers pointing to free throw line
TECHNICAL FOUL	**DOUBLE FOUL**	**INTENTIONAL FOUL**
Form T, Palm Showing	Waving clenched fists	Grasp wrist

CHARGING	**ILLEGAL USE OF HANDS**	**BLOCKING**
Clench fist striking open palm	Signal foul: strike wrist	Both hands on hips
FOUL BY TEAM IN CONTROL OF THE BALL	**TO DESIGNATE OFFENDER**	**TWO FREE THROWS**
Clenched fist towards basket of team committing the foul	Hold up number of player	Fingers together
ONE FREE THROW	**THREE FREE THROWS**	**ONE AND ONE PENALTY**
Close hand with pointed index finger	Three pointed fingers (thumb, index and middle fingers)	Index finger

The scorer

The scorer's equipment consists of an official score sheet, a signal (horn or bell) and five markers numbered 1 to 5.

The scorer is required to:

● record the names and numbers of all players taking part in a game, and inform the nearest official if there is any breach of the rules regarding the numbers and substitution of players

- keep a chronological running summary of the points scored by each team
- note all fouls, personal and technical, and tell an official immediately when a player has committed a total of five fouls, or a team has committed a total of seven fouls
- indicate the number of fouls committed by each player by raising the appropriate numbered marker
- record the time-outs debited to each team, and warn a team through an official when it has taken a second time-out
- sound his signal when a substitution or charged time-out is requested.

The score sheet

The score sheet consists of three sheets: the original on white paper—this is for the organisers of the match; a copy on pink paper—for the winning team and a copy on gold paper—for the losing team.

Score

In each section there are five columns, the central one (shaded) being marked M. This central column is to indicate the time, in full minutes, starting with 1 and ending with 20 in each half. The time shall be inscribed only when necessary. The score for each team is recorded in the other columns, using the left-handed group of two columns for the team shooting in the bas-

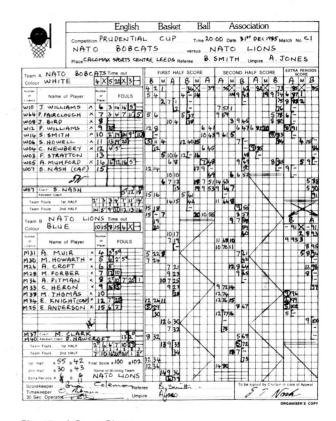

Fig. 17   A Score Sheet

ket which is to the left of the scorer's table, and the right-handed columns for the other team. The letters A and B shall be inscribed at the top after the teams have selected baskets. At the half-time interval the positions are reversed.

In each group of two columns (for each team), the first column is for the number of the player and the second for the total running score of that team. A field goal for 3 points is recorded by drawing a circle around the number of the player. A missed free throw shall be indicated with a short horizontal line. Free throws belonging to the same penalty shall be bracketed together. Only one score may be recorded on any one line; if team A scores the corresponding squares of team B shall remain blank.

Fouls

When a foul (personal or technical) is called against a player, the scorer shall indicate it by inscribing the time (in full minutes) in the appropriate square. The scorer shall indicate the award of free throws by adding an apostrophe after the minute, a technical foul by adding a capital T, and a disqualifying foul by adding a capital D. In the case of an intentional foul, the time shall be enclosed in a circle.

All fouls, up to 7 should also be indicated by inscribing the time in the appropriate square on the score sheet and so a record of team fouls in each half is kept.

Time-out

When a team requests and is granted a charged time-out, the scorer shall indicate it by inscribing the time (in full minutes) in the allotted section. There are two squares for each half and one square for each eventual extra period.

The timekeeper

The timekeeper's equipment consists of two stop-watches (a game watch and a time-out watch), and a signal (gong, horn, bell or pistol), which is different from the scorer's signal.

The timekeeper is required to:

● notify the referee more than 3 minutes before the start of each half, so that the referee can give the teams a clear 3 minutes warning before the game is to start
● record playing time
● time stoppages
● indicate the ending of playing time in each half or extra period by sounding his signal.

The game watch is started:

● if play is resumed by a jump ball, when the ball after reaching its highest point is tapped by the first player
● if a free throw is not successful and the ball is to continue in play, when the ball touches a player on the court

Fig. 18   Scoreboard and Clock

nent. Each player can shoot from any position on the playing court. The popularity of the game can be traced to this essential simplicity, which enables every player to do everything. Good players and leading teams are those who can perform the simple skills very well. Although the game is simple to play, to master it requires practice on the part of individual players and the team.

Playing positions

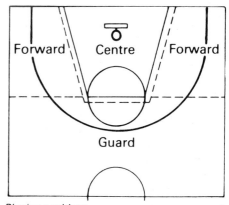

Fig. 19   Playing positions

● if play is resumed by a throw-in from out-of-bounds, when the ball touches a player on the court.

The game watch is stopped when an official signals a violation, a foul, a held ball, suspension of play for an injury, suspension of play for any reason by an official or when the 30 second signal sounds.

Advice on play

Basketball is a game of maximum participation; no player on either team is restricted from getting the ball whenever it is in play, and players are free to occupy any part of the playing area not occupied by an oppo-

The player's position in the team will depend upon his own skill, that of his team mates, his height in relation to other members of the team and the tactics the coach decides to use. In basketball the name given to the player's position is determined by the area of the court usually taken up when the team is on attack. There are three basic court playing positions: guard, forward and centre.

Guard

A player who plays in the guard position will, when his team is on attack, usually operate in the area of court between the centre line and the free-throw line extended to the side lines. He will usually be one of the smaller players on the team and will be responsible for bringing the ball up court to start the team's attack. A talented guard will be able to use his drive to move in close to the basket, not necessarily for a shot, but to draw the defence onto himself and then pass off to a team mate in a better position for the shot.

Forward

The forwards play on attack in the area of the court, either on the right- or left-hand side, between the restricted areas and the side lines. They will be among the taller players on the team, have a good drive and be able to shoot well from the corner and side of the court. If they are playing forward they must be prepared to move in to gain attacking rebounds should a shot be missed.

Centre

The player selected to play in the centre position is usually the tallest player in the team and plays on attack close to the basket. A centre will be expected to have the following skills: be a good shot close to basket (usually under pressure from close marking opponents), have the ability to get free to receive a pass and remain close to the basket and rebound strongly. The player in this position is occasionally referred to as a post or pivot player.

These playing positions are by no means rigid and as the team's attacking play develops so a guard may find himself playing from a forward position. However, an inexperienced player will find it easier to understand his role in the team's attack, if he is operating from a specific court position.

The number of players that a team uses in each position can be varied, and will depend upon the tactics selected by the team coach. The use of players by the coach will ensure a balanced spacing of the players in their front court.

Team play basics

To achieve the basic aim of the game both teams play a 'percentage' game. The team on attack endeavour to move the ball to a position from which they will have a high percentage chance of scoring, while the defensive team tries to stop the opponents gaining a position for a good shot, thereby trying to give the attacking team only the poor percentage shots, which are the long range shots and those taken by closely marked players.

Team play in basketball involves the application of ideas similar to those applied in other games and these are as follows.

Safe passing

Basketball being a no-contact sport, a team should find it relatively easy to retain possession of the ball. To do this they must:

- pass and catch with two hands
- use short range passes (3–4 m or 10–15 ft)

Fig. 20   Player signalling for the ball

- hold the ball ready prior to the pass—this is usually at chest height or above
- discourage the use of long range or lob passes
- have the receiver of the pass move free and signal to his team mate.

Spread out

On the limited area of a basketball court the team on attack should endeavour to spread out so there is 3–4 m (10–15 ft) between each attacking player. This makes it difficult for the one defender to mark two attackers, easy to make fast accurate passes and gives space between defenders for the attackers to move.

Movement and control

The basic attacking play in basketball should be a pass to a team mate and a movement towards the basket, looking for a return pass. Beginners and inexperienced players frequently attempt to play the game too fast and make too much movement. Basketball is a game of changes of tempo; play may be initially built up slowly and then rapid movement is made as a scoring chance is developed.

Basketball being a no-contact game, emphasis should be placed on controlled movements about the court. A player moves only when he has himself and the ball under control.

Individual play

The simplest **defence** used in the game is for a defensive player to be resonsible for one opponent, aiming to limit the attacking options of that player. The basic **attacking options** available to the player are to shoot, to drive (dribble past the opponent), to pass and to move. Before using any of these options the attacking player may make use of a fake. The basic defensive position should be taken up between the attacking player and the basket that is being defended, so that the attacking player has to dribble round the defender in order to take a close-to-basket shot. The defender will adjust his position, use his hands to discourage an easy shot or pass and his feet to prevent a dribbler from penetrating close to the basket.

Individual skills

Getting free

For most of the game a player on court will not have the ball. An important skill without the ball is getting free to receive a pass. To gain the advantage against the opponent to create space to receive, the player can:

(a) move towards the ball, or

(b) move away from the ball and then go back towards the ball, or

(c) move towards the basket and then move out to receive the ball.

When a change of direction is used to get free the player should also change speed, moving slowly at first, walking, and then running fast on the change of direction.

Catching

The receiver having moved free should:

● make a target with his hands for the passer to aim at
● keep his eyes on the ball
● receive the ball by catching it in two hands with the fingers spread and cushion it in by bending the arms
● endeavour to get the ball under control in two hands as quickly as possible, so he is ready to shoot, start a dribble or make a pass.

Shooting

Once the ball has been caught the attacking player should check if he is within scoring range. If not facing the goal, the player should endeavour to pivot immediately so as to look for the basket. If, when he faces the basket, there is no defender in line between him and the basket, he could dribble in and use a *lay-up* shot. Should the attacking player find he is within scoring range and the opponent is not close, but is in position between the ball and basket, the ball handler may use a *set* shot or a *jump* shot.

Lay-up shot

The essential ingredients of the shot are that it is taken on the move, usually on the run; the player jumps up and towards the basket as he shoots, and stretches to release the ball as close to the basket as possible. As the player moves forward and picks the ball up at the end of a dribble or after receiving a pass, he takes the ball in two hands, lifting his head as he gathers the ball so that he can look for the shot early. The diagram on the next page shows the ball being taken in the air with the player landing first on his right foot and then on his left foot, as he takes a long final step. This enables him to control his forward momentum and helps him to prepare for the high jump off the left foot. As he jumps off one foot, he carries the ball upwards, still in both hands. Notice that the take-off foot for the shot is the opposite to the shooting hand. The player releases the ball at full stretch from one hand, using the backboard to bank the ball into the basket.

Fig. 21   Lay-up shot

Set shot

Although this shot has limited use in the modern game, it may be used for distance shots should the defender sag off (see p. 39); it is also useful for young players. The player taking the set shot takes up a stride position with his feet, the same foot forward as the shooting hand. Prior to taking the shot he bends his knees slight-ly. The player looks at the basket throughout the shot. He follows through with a vigorous snap of the wrist and fingers, and, with the powerful drive from the legs, finishes the shot at full stretch.

Fig. 22   Set shot

Jump shot

This is perhaps the most effective shot in the modern game. The shot may be from a stationary position following a head or foot fake, after a pivot, after receiving a pass, or at the end of a dribble. The player aims to take off from both feet in a vertical direction. As he jumps the ball is taken up in front of his face to a position above the head with the shooting hand behind the ball, just in front of the forehead. The ball is released, near the top of the jump, with an upwards extension of the arm, and flipped towards the basket with a vigorous wrist and finger action.

When shooting, a player should concentrate on the following:

● look for the shot early, concentrating on the ring before, during, and after the shot
● hold the ball firmly in both hands with the fingers spread
● shoot the ball with one hand, with the wrist of the shooting hand fully extended before the shot
● shoot with a strong wrist and finger flick, following through with the wrist and fingers
● be on balance and under control during the shot; this enables a smooth follow-through which is essential for accuracy. Balance starts at the feet, so always establish a firm foot position before shooting.

Footwork

The stride and jump stop are illustrated on pages 9 and 10. The jump stop is particularly valuable as there is no commitment to a pivot foot on landing. As the landing has been made on both feet simultaneously, either foot may be selected to be the pivot foot depending upon the game situation. A pivot can be used by a player to establish balance, improve his position and create space for a shot.

Stops and the use of pivot should be used as part of a natural moving action, i.e. as part of a run or walk.

Dribbling

Because the dribble enables the player to move with the ball it is an essential skill to develop. In the dribble the player controls the ball by spreading the fingers comfortably, so that they contact as much of the ball as possible. The ball is pushed down firmly using hand, elbow and wrist. The dribbling hand should be on top of the ball. This will prevent 'palming' and ensure that the ball rebounds to the hand accurately. Once the player has mastered the touch of the dribble he must dribble by feel only, so that he can at the same time see movements by team mates and opponents. Some inexperienced players get into the habit of bouncing the ball once every time they receive a pass. This prevents another dribble and it limits the individual attacking movements of these players. A skilled basketball player is able to dribble equally well with either hand, to change direction and speed. It is through these manoeuvres that he can beat an opponent. Dribbling the ball towards the basket in an attempt to beat an opponent and take a shot is called a drive.

Fig. 23   Dribble past opponent

The drive

The drive will be used by an attacking player to beat a defender who makes a mistake. These are likely to be mistakes in balance relative to the attacking player and the basket. The man mistakes are:

- moving towards the attacking player. This is the mistake most commonly made by beginners who, after the man they are marking has received a pass and is facing the basket, rush towards him. In this situation they can be easily caught off balance and beaten with a drive
- jumping up to check an anticipated shot. While the defender is going up, the attacking player can drive round him for basket.
- moving backwards towards the basket. This gives the attacking player time and space for a shot
- movements laterally—left or right. If the defensive player is to the attacker's left the drive can be made to the right.

To cause the defender to make one of these mistakes a fake may be necessary. For example, a player facing the goal and looking up towards the basket can find that the defender thinks that a shot is about to be taken and moves. Movements laterally can be caused by the use of a foot fake before the start of a dribble, or, if the attacking player is already dribbling, by the use of a change of direction and change hands dribble.

Passing

To be effective a pass must be taken by the receiver *when* and *where* he wants it and the importance of timing the pass and placing it in relation to the position of the receiver should be stressed. Passing involves two players, the passer and the receiver, and getting free to receive a pass has been covered on p. 30. The passer must be able to make accurate passes so that the receiver can become an immediate triple threat, i.e. can shoot, drive or pass. A skilled passer should try to be deceptive, disguising his intentions by not staring at the team mate and not winding-up. Passes should be quick and firm, with a quick release of the ball preferable to a fast, hard movement through the air. The fast pass that requires a preparatory wind-up will give the opponents a chance to anticipate the pass. The passer will also need to appreciate the relative positions and movements being made by opponents and team mates.

The main passes used in the game are:

Chest pass

This is the most important and basic pass of the game used for fast accurate passing at short range. From a position with the ball held in two hands at the chest with the fingers alongside the ball and thumbs behind, pass the ball by fully extending the arms, snapping the wrist and pushing the ball with the fingers. Relax the elbows and extend the arms to follow through fully.

Fig. 24   Chest pass

Two hand overhead pass

This is an excellent pass for the taller player to use when passing over a smaller player. The ball is taken up in two hands to a position above the head (see Fig. 26) and from this position it is passed with a vigorous snap of the wrist and fingers directly to a team mate.

Hand-off pass

When a team mate is cutting close to the ball handler, a short hand-off pass is used. In this pass the ball is put into the air, so that the cutting player can take the ball as soon as possible after the ball leaves the passer's hand.

Other passes may be made via the floor. These bounce passes are slower and have only limited use in the game.

Individual defence

A player's responsibility in defence againt an opponent may be listed as follows:

- discourage the opponent from shooting from a high-percentage scoring area
- anticipate his moves so as to discourage him driving past for a shot from closer to basket
- make it difficult for the opponent to pass accurately, particularly passes into the high-percentage scoring area
- make it difficult for him to run past to receive a pass or collect a rebound.

Individual defence against a dribbler

To be able to defend, an individual usually takes a defensive position between opponent and the basket. If the opponent is in a shooting position, the defender should be close enough to discourage the shot; should the opponent be away from the ball, the defender can sag off him (see p. 39) towards the basket he is defending, changing his stance so as to be able to see the opponent and the ball. To maintain this position the defender needs a stance with knees slightly flexed and head up, with feet flat on the floor and spread approximately shoulder-width apart with one foot in front of the other. This stance enables the defender to make quick movements; the footwork used is a sliding action. Try not to cross the feet so that rapid changes of direction can be made. The hands and arms play an important part in defence. They can be used to maintain balance and discourage offensive shooting, driving or passing.

Good defence is played with the two ends of the body, the feet and the brain. The defender needs to analyse his opponent's moves, his strengths and weaknesses, so as to be able to anticipate and reduce the attacking player's potential options. For example, can his opponent only dribble successfully with one hand or does he have a favourite shooting position? If he is a potential pass receiver then the defender may adjust his position and place a hand in the passing lane to discourage the pass.

Movement

Once a player has passed the ball he should look for opportunities to move to receive a return pass. One of the basic attacking moves in the game is the 'Give and Go'. A player 'gives' – passes the ball to a team mate – then 'goes' – cuts to basket looking for a return pass.

Give and go

Any two players on court can work together in this way, with a player taking advantage of a mistake by his opponent to cut free, or make a fake, e.g. a change of direction to beat his opponent. In the game, the Give and Go is usually used either between two guards or, more likely, between a guard and a forward. In this latter move the guard passes ahead to a forward and then cuts for basket for the return pass. Playing against an inexperienced defender the player who passes ahead, as in a guard-to-forward move, may find that the defender is tempted to turn to see where the ball has gone; at this moment the attacking player is free and should immediately cut for basket, signalling for the return pass. To make the immediate cut, a player needs to be well balanced, with knees flexed so as to be able to make the quick start that will enable the play to get past the opponent. Should the opponent not make an error, it can be forced by using a change of direction and pace to beat him, as in Fig. 26.

Fig. 26   Give and go

Simple team tactics for beginners

Team defence

The simplest and easiest defence to play is man-to-man; each defender is assigned to mark a specific opponent regardless of where he goes in his offensive manoeuvres. Defenders will need to concentrate on the opponent rather than the ball. If the attacking opponent is a long way from the basket or the ball a defender may sag, i.e. move away from his opponent towards the basket he is defending.

Fig. 27   Attack versus man-to-man defence

Team attack

Again simplicity is required. This can be achieved by spreading out the attacking players as shown below and by working as indivduals or in pairs to create a scoring opportunity. Each individual player when he receives the ball can check through his options — **shot—drive—pass—move**.

The pass and move involve the team mate, and the Give and Go (see Fig. 26) is a simple two-player move.

A simple team tactic could be stated as:

Look ahead — face the basket you are attacking particularly when you are holding the ball

Pass ahead
Move ahead — on gaining possession quickly start an attack by moving the ball ahead – fast break

— cut to basket after a pass

— drive to basket

— get free ahead of the team mate holding the ball

Spread out — so as to keep space between team mates and to leave the under-basket area clear

Control — most of the game is played without the ball, move to help a team mate. Think before you move, maybe the best thing to do is stand still.

Index